FOLENS
PHOTOPACK
ANCIENT EGYPT

Les Ray

Folens
Publishers

INTRODUCTION

The purpose of this photopack is to provide teachers and children with strong visual images of Ancient Egypt, with suggested activities to stimulate discussion and personal research. These will give some insight into the way of life, beliefs and achievements of an ancient culture which continues to hold a strong fascination for both young and old.

This photopack should be used alongside other sources from today and other times in the past in order to help children understand the concept of change – both rapid and gradual – and in learning about different features of the period they will understand that historical events usually have more than one cause and consequence.

Two important issues need to be addressed:

● 'Ancient Egypt' covers a huge time span, from King Narmer of the First Dynasty (3100BC) to Cleopatra and the division of the Roman Empire in AD395. Children need to be made aware of this time span. A visual way of doing this is by using a kitchen roll as a timeline, each section representing one century. Children will then be able to appreciate that some of the objects and buildings shown in this pack are over 4 000 years old. Children could add other events in history to sections of the timeline.

● The study of Egypt offers numerous opportunities to use both primary and secondary sources. In using secondary sources, children should be encouraged to explore different interpretations, e.g. historians might disagree about the dates, the Egyptian way of life might be portrayed in different ways, was Tutankhamun murdered? Children should come to understand that often it is the deficiency of evidence which leads to different interpretations. A deeper understanding of this is that the historian's selection of sources and the attitudes he/she might hold further influences the interpretation. It is essential therefore that children meet a variety of interpretations.

NB. The photographs can be used for research, e.g. *What is it? How was it used?* To facilitate this, the description of each photograph is in the teacher's notes and not on the photograph.

First published 1993 by Folens Limited.
United Kingdom: Folens Publishers, Apex Business Centre, Boscombe Road, Dunstable, LU5 4RL.
Email: folens@folens.com

Ireland: Folens Publishers, Greenhills Road, Tallaght, Dublin 24.
Email: info@folens.ie

Poland: JUKA, ul. Renesansowa 38, Warsaw 01-905

Folens allows photocopying of pages marked 'copiable page' for educational use, providing that this use is within the confines of the purchasing institution. Copiable pages should not be declared in any return in respect of any photocopying licence.

Cover: In Touch Creative Service Ltd   Cover photo: © Michael Holford   Illustrations: Barrie Richardson

The author and publisher would like to thank the following for permission to reproduce the following photographs:
Page 3 Funerary model of a ploughing scene. British Museum. Photo © Michael Holford.
Page 4 Nakhte and his wife in a garden. Papyrus now in the British Museum. Photo © Michael Holford.
Page 5 The Pyramids at Giza. Photo © Michael Holford.
Page 6 The Rosetta Stone. British Museum. Photo © Michael Holford.
Page 7 The mask of Tutankhamun. Photo © C M Dixon.
Page 8 The tomb of Sennedjem. Photo © Ancient Art and Architecture Collection.
Page 9 Entrance to the temple at Luxor – obelisk and statues of Ramesses II. Photo © Ancient Art and Architecture Collection.
Page 10 Abu Simbel. Temple of Ramses II. Photo © Ancient Art and Architecture Collection.
Page 11 A wooden board game from Ancient Egypt. Photo © Ancient Art and Architecture Collection.
Page 12 The judgement of Ani. Papyrus now in the British Museum. Photo © Michael Holford.

© 1993 Folens Limited, on behalf of the author.

Every effort has been made to contact copyright holders of material used in this publication. If any copyright holder has been overlooked, we should be pleased to make any necessary arrangements.

British Library Cataloguing in Publication Data. A catalogue record for this publication is available from the British Library.
ISBN 185276 526-7

FARMING

Funerary model of a ploughing scene. British Museum. Photo © Michael Holford.

The River Nile is essential to life in Egypt. Agriculture would not have been possible without the annual flooding (inundation). The level of the inundation was crucial. If there was not enough water, the ground could not produce sufficient crops for the next season. If there was too much water, severe damage could be caused and land would be too wet to plant crops.

Nilometers recorded water levels along the river. Priests used the previous year's records to estimate the level of flood.

All land was owned by the Pharaoh. Staple crops grown were barley, wheat and flax. Gardens produced fruits, green vegetables, beans and grapes. Meat was a luxury, but cattle, pigs, goats, ducks and geese were reared.

The photograph shows a shabti from about 2000BC. In the afterlife it was possible that Osiris might expect a person to do manual work. Pharaohs, priests and priestesses had shabtis buried with them in their tombs. These were believed to jump to life at the command of Osiris and would do the work. Some people were buried with hundreds of shabtis.

Starting points

◆ Children should look carefully at the picture and describe what they see.
◆ Ask children to write down three statements which they can deduce from the picture.
◆ Ask the children what else they would like to find out about farming in Ancient Egypt. Write down three questions.
◆ How could they find out the answers to these questions?

Activities

● Explain to the children that the photograph is of a shabti. They could design and make shabtis which they would wish to have buried with them. These should reflect the jobs they would not wish to do in the afterlife. Children can guess what they are.

● Explain to the children how the priests used a Nilometer to forecast the annual flooding. A Nilometer was usually built within temples, e.g. Edfu. Steps went down into the ground. The level of the Nile was marked each month. Priests would look at the level and compare it with the same month the previous year. If it were higher they would expect more flooding than the previous year. If it were lower they would expect less. Their predictions were quite accurate.

● Ask the children to think of reasons why the priests predicted the level of flood and told the people that the gods were pleased or not with them. How might the priests control the actions of people during the future year if they believed this?

● The silt transported by the Nile was deposited on the land when the floods came. This kept the land fertile from year to year.

● Dissolve some soil in a bottle of water. Shake it up and leave it to settle to give the idea of suspension of particles in water. Strain the liquid through fine mesh or filter paper to show how silt would have been left on the land when waters receded.

● Draw calendars for display of the Ancient Egyptian farming year.

● Which crops is it possible to grow in such areas? Can we grow them in our country? If not, why not?

● Compare farming in Egypt today. What things have stayed the same? What differences are there? Why?

3

HOUSES

Nakht and his wife in a garden (Papyrus). British Museum. Photo © Michael Holford.

Scenes like this from Books of the Dead and from tomb paintings provide us with interesting historical sources about domestic life in Ancient Egypt. However, art of this kind was not simply historical record and so care must be taken with interpretation, e.g. Books of the Dead gave advice for the afterlife and so tried to show the characters in their best light.

We do know that houses were mostly built from mud brick and so little has survived. There was also a great variety of housing. The workmen's village at El-Amarna consisted of seventy-two small units, measuring 5m by 10m. Animals lived in one of the two rooms, the other was a living and sleeping area. In the tiny kitchen area of this room was a stairway to the flat roof, also used for sleeping and cooking. This picture (c. 1340BC) shows a more prosperous house, of Nakht a scribe - an important man in the bureaucracy of Ancient Egypt. He is in his garden, with his wife, worshipping Osiris. This is from his Book of the Dead, once in his tomb but now in the British Museum.

Starting points

◆ Children should look carefully at the picture and describe what they think is happening.
◆ Why did Nakht have an image of himself and his wife worshipping Osiris painted?
◆ What else would the children like to find out about houses or domestic life in Ancient Egypt. Write down three questions.
◆ How could they find out the answers to these questions?

Activities

● Did scientific/geographical factors affect people's behaviour in the past?
● Discuss the inundation and its importance. Why is the house built on a platform?
● Ask children to count the windows high up in the house and comment on their size. Why are they not larger and lower to let the maximum light in?
● Why is the house painted white? Can children think of experiments to show that white reflects the light and heat?
● What are the peculiar shapes on the roof?
● Talk about how hot air would rise through the vents and cooler air would be taken in through the windows, thus ensuring circulation of air.

● Make a 3D model of the house in card or clay and paint it appropriately.
● Would all houses in Egypt have had pillars? What would they have been like? Research designs used on Egyptian pillars.
● There is no attempt at perspective in this picture. Do we draw in this way now? If not, why not?
● Draw the pool and its trees flat, cut out the shape and bend the trees up to show how shady it must have been with all the trees overlooking it. Place beside the model.

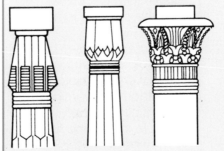

● Consider the plan of the house at Deir el-Medina, information about El-Amarna and the picture. Is the model an accurate version of an Ancient Egyptian house?
● Films tend to give us the view that Ancient Egyptians all lived in grand monumental buildings (see pages 5 and 9). Is this a correct interpretation?

PYRAMIDS

The Pyramids at Giza.
Photo © Michael Holford.

The pyramid tombs at Giza were constructed between 2589 and 2530BC by three of the rulers of the 4th Dynasty - Cheops, Chephren and Mycerinus. They were built of limestone with a facing of finer limestone. Much of the facing material has now disappeared.

The Great Pyramid was originally 146m in height, each side at the base measured 230m, the angle of the sides was 51° 50 to the base. An estimated 2 300 000 stones were used. It is believed they were built in this shape because they pointed the way to the sun for the souls buried in them. They are not isolated monuments but are the focus of a complex of surrounding buildings - smaller tombs and ceremonial mortuary temples and the Sphinx. Burial chambers are deep within and are reached by long, narrow, steep passages. Most of the chambers were empty when opened - they had already been robbed.

Herodotus wrote that they had been built by slaves, but we now know that they were built by conscripted labour during inundation when no work could be done on the land.

Starting points

- Children should look carefully at the picture and describe what they see.
- Why do they think the three smaller pyramids are called 'step pyramids'?
- Grave robbers emptied the tombs. Ask children to make a list of the artefacts they might have removed.
- Ask the children what else they would like to find out about pyramids in Ancient Egypt.
- What sources might help them?

Activities

- The historian Herodotus influenced many people's interpretation of history for centuries. Read the source and look at the picture. Write down statements about the monument which are facts and points of view.
- The Ancient Egyptians used the cubit as a measure. What do we use today? This was based on the average distance between a man's elbow and the end of his middle finger, equivalent to 0.46m. Measure the room using individual children's cubits and then convert the figures to those of today.
- Just how big are the pyramids? Would one fit into the school grounds?

'Cheops compelled everyone without exception to serve as slaves to his own end ... a hundred thousand men in a shift ... to build his pyramid took ten years ...'

Herodotus 460BC

A - King's Chamber
B - Queen's Chamber
C - Unfinished Chamber

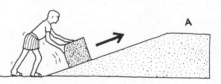

- How did the Ancient Egyptians build these monuments? Large pieces of stone had to be moved up the side of a slope.

- How could this be done easily? Why would **A** be easier than **B**? What would make **A** even easier?
- Ask the children to make simple rollers and use them to move objects. Why did the Egyptians not use wheels?

WRITING

The Rosetta Stone. British Museum. Photo © Michael Holford.

The Rosetta Stone was found at Rosetta in 1799 by a French soldier. It records messages by High Priests to Ptolemy V in about 196BC, and is written in hieroglyphs (top), demotic (popular) Egyptian (middle) and Greek capitals (bottom). It took 20 years work by Francois Champollion to find the key to the symbols. **Hieroglyph** comes from the Greek - Hieros (sacred) and Glupho (sculpture).

Education in Ancient Egypt was mainly vocational - children learned the trades of their fathers. It is estimated that ninety-eight per cent of the people were illiterate. Scribes were not just the writers; they were accountants, and recorders of State affairs: 'If you know how to write, it will serve you better than any other position,' states an Ancient Egyptian proverb.

Interest in hieroglyphic script dates back even to the Greek historian Herodotus in the fourth century BC:

'... they go from right to left and maintain that theirs is the best method, ours being left-handed and clumsy.' Ancient Egyptians had little access to tree pulp for paper. They did have papyrus reeds in the marshy ground of the Nile Valley. The spongy pith from the stalks was sliced thinly and pressed together to form writing material.

Starting points

- ◆ Children should look carefully at the picture and describe what they see.
- ◆ The first word to be translated was PTOLEMYS. Ask the children to use page 16 and write this name in hieroglyphs.
- ◆ It took many years after Champollion to work out what every hieroglyph meant. Ask the children to list the consequences of being able to read hieroglyphs after all those centuries.

Activities

- ● Explain to the children how difficult it was to transcribe the hieroglyphs of Ancient Egypt without knowledge of the thousands of small pictures.
- ● Give them codes to break and ask them to make up codes of their own. How much help do they need before things become obvious?
- ● Ask them to copy some of the hieroglyphs and see if they can recognise any using page 16. Comparison with the Ancient Greek alphabet may help identify similar words.
- ● Look at other pictures in this pack that contain hieroglyphics. What are they written on? Is this the same as the Rosetta Stone?
- ● How is it that some writing has survived as historical evidence and some has not?
- ● Why did the Egyptians not have paper as we do? Investigate how we make paper today and how papyrus was made.

- ● All Egyptian Pharaohs recorded their names for posterity and the afterlife in stone within oblong shapes called cartouches.
- ● Children can use page 16 to create their own cartouches. These can be made large and displayed.

Tutankhamun

A scribe's portable kit

Two small flat slates for grinding pigments into ink
Dishes for mixing inks with water
Stones to smooth and scrape off the surface of papyrus
Reeds for brushes
Small wooden boxes for the hard cakes of ink

- ● Discuss how the objects in this box would have been used. Draw what they think the objects would look like.

6

TUTANKHAMUN

The mask of Tutankhamun. Photo © C M Dixon.

Tutankhamun, the most famous Pharaoh known to us made little impact during his short reign - 1347 to 1338BC (N.B. opinions vary). Originally named Tutankhaten, it is thought he was the son of Akhenaten who has become known as the 'heretic king'. Akhenaten moved the capital to el-Amarna from Thebes. He introduced the worship of one god - Aten. Temples of other gods were closed and the name of Amun - god of Thebes was erased from all monuments. Tutankhaten was a puppet Pharaoh. He married his half sister Ankhesanaten (daughter of Nefertiti) and succeeded to the throne at the age nine. Tutankhaten and his wife's names were changed to Tutankhamun and Ankhesenamun and the capital moved back to Thebes. The god Amun was reinstated and the name of Akhenaten erased.

The tomb of Tutankhamun was discovered by Howard Carter in 1922. Grave robbers had been there before him, but much of the treasure was intact.

The golden and lapis lazuli mask was found on the mummy inside the three golden coffins. It is now with the rest of the treasure from the tomb in the Egyptian Museum, Cairo.

Starting points

◆ Children should look carefully at the photograph and say how old they think the Pharaoh was.
◆ Akhenaten had been a threat to priests and officials who ruled through temples and gods. Tutankhaten was a puppet Pharaoh as a child. Power was in the hands of Aya, the chief official and later general Haremhab. Children should consider the motives of these two people.
◆ How did they benefit from having a young Pharaoh?
◆ Why might the Pharaoh have been killed when he was eighteeen?

Activities

● Many stories have built up around Tutankhamun - a curse on his tomb, a heroic boy King, murdered by a blow to the head.
● How can we find out how much of this is fact and how much fiction?

Medical report on body
1.65m long, large incision in stomach. Bones not fully grown; age about 18-20; clean shaven, white-skinned; ears small and pierced; nose broken, packed with linen; teeth large, wisdom teeth just through.

● Compared with the mask what extra useful information does the medical report give us?
● Children are fascinated by the mummy. Investigate decay and preservation of organic materials and how and why the Ancient Egyptians tried to preserve themselves. (See also pages 8 and 12.)

● Masks were true likenesses of the dead as the spirit would have to recognise the person in order to return to the body (see page 8).
● Use papier mâché over a balloon or use wet tissue and parcel tape over a face to build up features. Decorate the mask when dry.
● Add the NEMES - the striped head-dress, a beard (strapped on) and the royal symbols of Upper and Lower Egypt - the vulture and the cobra.
● Wearing the mask children can explain why it was so important for Kings to wear both symbols. (See page 10.)
● Was it easy to make a good likeness? What problems would Egyptian craftsmen have had making a gold mask?
● Women were also Pharaohs. Queen Hapsetshut wore a false beard, as did all Pharaohs, as a symbol of royalty!
● Use the plan of the tomb on page 15 to help research where all the various objects were found. Use the scale to enlarge the picture and make a large class plan.

TOMBS

The tomb of Sennedjem. Photo © Ancient Art and Architecture Collection.

Tombs were houses for the dead, decorated and furnished to create a proper environment for the person to pass eternity. Tomb paintings and reliefs provide a wealth of information about the lives of ordinary people. Although only the top stratum of society were buried in tombs, the decorated walls show scenes of different aspects of life. These are supplemented by tomb models 'shabtis' and objects of daily use which often form part of funerary equipment. This tomb wall painting is from about 280BC. The setting is the mythical Fields of Ialu (reeds) where Sennedjem and his wife Iyneferti are shown reaping grain, ploughing with a pair of dappled cattle and harvesting flax. Only the heads of grain were cut off with a short-handled wooden sickle, the blade of which was formed of sharp flakes of flint. The remaining much valued straw was pulled up later. To ensure immortality, Ancient Egyptians believed that all the different elements of human life had to survive.

Starting points

◆ Children should look carefully at the picture and describe what is happening.
◆ It is unlikely that Sennedjem and his wife would want to work in the fields. What might they take with them to ensure this didn't happen?
◆ What other scenes can the children recognise in the painting? (Opening of the mouth, boat journey to the afterlife).

Activities

● What was the purpose of decorating tombs? The picture shows an agricultural scene on a tomb wall.
● Why do children think it was painted in a tomb?
● If they then know that Ancient Egyptians believed their afterlife was spent in an agricultural world called the Fields of Reeds, does this make a difference to their interpretation?
● Is this picture a factual representation of life in Ancient Egypt, or was there a reason for the artist not to be truthful?
● Look at other pictures found in tombs or in Books of the Dead on pages 4, 12. Do they have any features in common?
● Shabtis were small clay figures put into the tombs to help the dead do all the jobs necessary in the afterlife.
● What kinds of work would the dead need doing for them?
● Make shabtis out of clay and decorate them. Compare with shabti - see page 3.

● The tombs were narrow and dark. How was the artwork carried out? If the work was near to the tomb entrance they used reflections from large metal mirrors.
● Carry out experiments to show how much light present day mirrors can reflect. How far will the light travel?
● Deeper inside tombs small oil lights were used. What problem could these cause?
● How did the artists avoid the ceilings of the tombs being covered with soot?
● Make some simple oil lamps out of clay. Use rag wicks and varieties of cooking oil to see which contain most impurities when burned.
● Many tomb walls were carved and not painted.
● Choose an Egyptian symbol, e.g. the ankh sign or the eye of Horus. Carve it out of the flat surface of a cut potato first in relief, i.e. carve out the shape of the symbol itself.
● Secondly make the symbol stand proud, i.e. carve out all around the symbol.
● Which was easier and quicker? Are there any advantages to carving rather than painting?

MONUMENTS

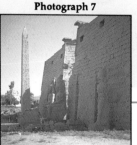

Entrance to the temple at Luxor. Photo © Ancient Art and Architecture Collection.

What remains of Ancient Egypt tends to be the magnificent monuments built by the Pharaohs for their gods to dwell and be worshipped in. The general rule was that temples and tombs were built of stone and houses and palaces were built of sun dried mud brick. For this reason there is little evidence remaining of the places people lived.

Major buildings like the Temple of Luxor in the picture (c. 1250BC) were constructed from Aswan granite and sandstone. The photograph gives some indication of the grandeur of the entrance, showing statues of Ramesses II (see page 10) and the remaining obelisk.

The pillar was used extensively in temple building. The Hypostyle Hall at Karnak has 134 enormous columns very close together rising to 22m. Labour was conscripted during the inundation when land could not be worked. People saw it as their duty to work for their Pharaoh.

Starting points

◆ Children should look carefully at the photograph and describe what they think has been removed.
◆ What would this site have looked like in the past? How and why has the building changed?
◆ Who might have removed statues and other monuments? Why?
◆ Children should discuss the issues involved in other countries being asked to return Egyptian treasure from their museums to Egypt.

Activities

● Make some mud bricks. Use straw in some and not in others. Leave them to dry out.
● Carry out experiments to test the strength of the mud bricks - with and without straw. Which is the stronger? Why?
● Does this explain why there is little evidence remaining of homes in which people lived?
● Compare with the building on page 4. Discuss the belief that all Egyptians lived in places like Luxor. Where did this interpretation come from? What evidence is there to prove it wrong?
● What technology did the Egyptians possess to raise and move large, heavy stones?
● Locate Aswan and Luxor on a map. (See page 13.) How was the granite moved to Luxor?
● How was the granite obelisk raised? Remember it's weight. It is 29.5m tall.
● How was it moved on the ground? Investigate the principle of rollers.

● Use the map of Edfu temple on page 14. Label the various sections with new Egyptian vocabulary - pylon, hypostyle hall, etc.
● The photograph shows the first pylon. What shape is it? Why is this a good shape for such a tall, thick wall?
● Note the holes at the top of the wall. These contained clamps into which went enormous flag poles.
● Children can build models of the temples, to scale if possible, to show their extent. Every stage was on a different level and the whole focus narrowed down to the sanctuary, the highest point, the house of the god.
● What were the particular rooms used for?

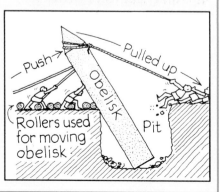
Push → Pulled up
Obelisk
Rollers used for moving obelisk
Pit

KINGSHIP

Abu Simbel. Temple of Ramesses II. Photo © Ancient Art and Architecture Collection.

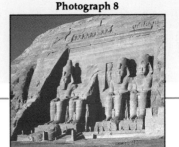

The Pharaoh was a god, a divine force, the centre of the country. He ruled in the place of Ra, the sun. All peoples were subject to the King; everything was owned by the King. He was the keeper of divine and temporal order, the warrior and the builder of temples to the gods.

The size and scale of the Temple of Abu Simbel, built by Ramesses II (1279-1213BC) shows the power of the Pharaohs. Cut out of solid rock it tells of the aspirations of a King who built more monuments to himself than any other. When the rising waters of Lake Nasser threatened the temple, it was decided to move it to a new location. In 1964, under the auspices of UNESCO, West German, Italian, French and Swedish engineers began work. The whole temple was dismantled and re-erected inside a concrete shell. It was reopened in 1968 and cost $40 million.

The four seated colossi of Ramesses II (each 20m high) each wears the double crown signifying the unity of Upper and Lower Egypt.

Starting points

◆ Children should look carefully at the picture and describe what they see. (The wives of Ramesses II are by his feet.)
◆ Ask children to write down three statements which can be deduced from the picture.
◆ Ask the children what else they would like to find out about Pharaohs in Ancient Egypt. Write down three questions.
◆ How could they find out the answers to these questions?
◆ Why was it important to move the temple in 1964?

Activities

● How do you recognise a King of both Kingdoms? By his crown and by what is on it!
● Make some shaped crowns out of card. Compare with ones in the photograph and in other pictures in this pack. Why use cobras and vultures as symbols?
● Why was it so important for Kings to be seen wearing both crowns?
● How large is Egypt? Draw a large map on a classroom wall (see page 13).
● What is the distance between Aswan and the delta?
● Interview Ramesses II. What problems would Kings have in defending their country?
● Why did he build such a large monument to himself?
● What were his attitudes to government?

Upper Egypt white crown (hedet) vulture symbol (neknbet)

Lower Egypt red crown (deset) cobra symbol (wadjet)

● Government was simple but was essential in order to keep such a large country together.
● Which was the most powerful group second to the Pharaoh?

Government in Ancient Egypt

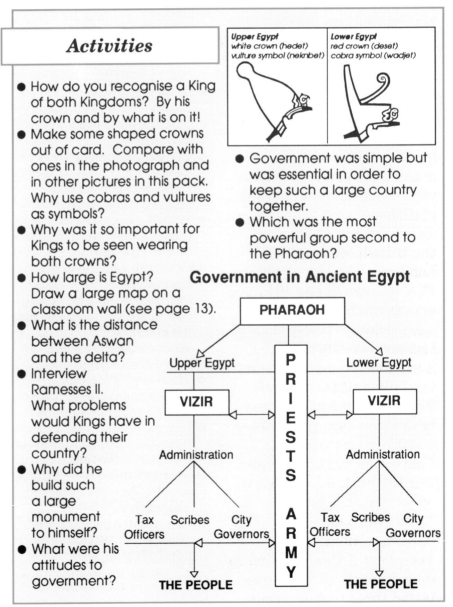

LEISURE

A wooden board game.
Photo © Ancient Art and
Architecture Collection.

Ancient Egypt was not just a civilisation concerned with death, religion and building monuments. Evidence from tombs, papyrus and from workmen's villages indicates how Ancient Egyptians spent their leisure time. Tomb paintings depict the Egyptian's concept of the afterlife (see pages 3 and 8). This was a continuation of the positive and enjoyable aspects of life on earth. It can be said that it was the enjoyment that they found in their 'ordinary' lives which made them want to continue it after death. Pictures of hunting abound; games, sports, dining and music were popular. The picture here shows a popular wooden board game called *senet* to be found in the British Museum, London.

The calendar of the ordinary person consisted of an eight day working week broken by two or three day holidays. Sixty-five days every year were allowed for festivals. These were religious in nature but celebration was joyous and frenzied. At Thebes the most important was the Festival of Opet, in which the gods (statues) Amun, Isis and Horus sailed down the Nile from the Temple at Karnak to Thebes (now Luxor). Celebrations lasted three to four weeks.

Starting points

◆ Children should look carefully at the picture and describe the game.
◆ Would the game be carried around? How do you know? How many players might have played it? Do we have similar games today?
◆ Ask the children what else they would like to find out about how Ancient Egyptians spent their leisure time. Write down three questions.
◆ How could they find out the answers to these questions?
◆ Does this photograph break any stereotyped views about the way that Ancient Egyptians lived, e.g. 'All work and no play'?
◆ Do the children think that all Egyptians would have enjoyed all the leisure activities? They should give reasons for their answers.

Activities

● Make up rules for the game and try to play it. It has thirty squares and uses different shaped pieces.
● Design some pieces in the shapes of different gods to play the game.
● Children can make their own versions.
● Egyptians enjoyed dining and feasting. Children can research what Egyptians would have eaten at such events (see page 3). How and why is this recipe for Ancient Egyptian bread different from bread today?

Recipe
4 cups wholemeal flour
half tsp salt
2 cups tepid water
Mix all together.
Knead for 5 minutes
Shape into a round
Leave for 24 hours

To cook put on baking tray in oven
30 mins Gas 4, Electric 350F, 180C

● Work was hard so leisure time was very important. What jobs would 'ordinary' people have done in Ancient Egypt?
● Egyptians enjoyed music and dancing. Ask the children to research:
  - musical instruments. Were any similar to those used today?
  - dance. Who danced? What did they wear? Did they dance in groups or individually?
● Egyptians also enjoyed gymnastic displays. Can the children find out about them?
● Many other toys have been found. These range from balls to toys with moveable parts.
● Design and make a toy with moveable parts, e.g. the jaws, for a young child. Use an Egyptian figure or idea as the basis.
● Why are there no toys on wheels until late in Ancient Egyptian history?

RELIGION

The judgement of Ani (Papyrus). British Museum. Photo © Michael Holford.

Religion and religious beliefs were central to life in Ancient Egypt. There seem to be a bewildering array of gods, but this is mostly due to the fact that the role of the deity changes over time.

Central to the belief is that the Sun (Atum - the All) is the creator. The Pharaoh is the representation of this god and his function is to keep the divine order in motion and to keep chaos at bay.

This picture shows the weighing of the heart ceremony from the Papyrus Book of the Dead of Ani (c.1250BC) in the British Museum, London. Anubis, the guardian of the land of the dead, is weighing the person's heart against a feather to see if sins in the real world were so significant that he was not fit to join Osiris.

Across the top, forty-two gods and goddesses sit in judgement. The 'Devourer' sits patiently waiting for the judgement. If the heart is heavy with sin, Ani will be denied access to the afterlife and fall victim to the Devourer.

Little is known about funerary practices of ordinary people as only Pharaohs, nobles and priests were buried in tombs.

Starting points

- Children should look carefully at the picture and describe what they see.
- Ask children to write down three statements commenting on what they have deduced from the picture. They should ask themselves, 'How do I know?', 'How did I find out?'
- Ask the children what else they would like to find out about religion in Ancient Egypt. Write down three questions.
- How could they find out the answers to these questions?

Activities

- What gods did the Ancient Egyptians believe in?
- What gods do we believe in today?
- What differences do we notice between the various religions of today?
- What gods can the children identify from the picture by their head-dresses?
- Wall paintings show the difficulties the soul had in trying to reach Osiris in the afterworld.
- Make up a board game to illustrate the tests and difficulties - serpents, crocodiles, traps, Anubis weighing your heart, etc.
- Stories and creation myths can be scripted and dramatised and compared with those of other religions, e.g. the battle for good and evil between Horus and Seth, the search for the remains of Osiris by Isis.
- Create a shadow play using the shapes of the gods and a sarcophagus to show the body being buried (perhaps in a pyramid shape).

- The picture shows Anubis weighing the person's heart against a feather. If the person had been evil the heart would not balance and the person would be turned away.
- Make a balance to illustrate the scientific principle. Experiment with different weights.
- Does the balance always have to have equal weights to balance?
- Create mobiles from cut-outs of the shapes of various gods usually recognisable by their individual head-dresses.
- Does the string from which the figures hang always have to be the same length? What about the rods?
- Demonstrate knowledge of the gods by producing a large wall display. Cut a large pyramid out of paper and cut small windows in it.
- Paste the pictures of the gods behind the windows to produce an 'advent calendar' effect.
- Children can label the outsides of the windows. Others have to describe the god inside and open the window to see if correct.

ANCIENT EGYPT

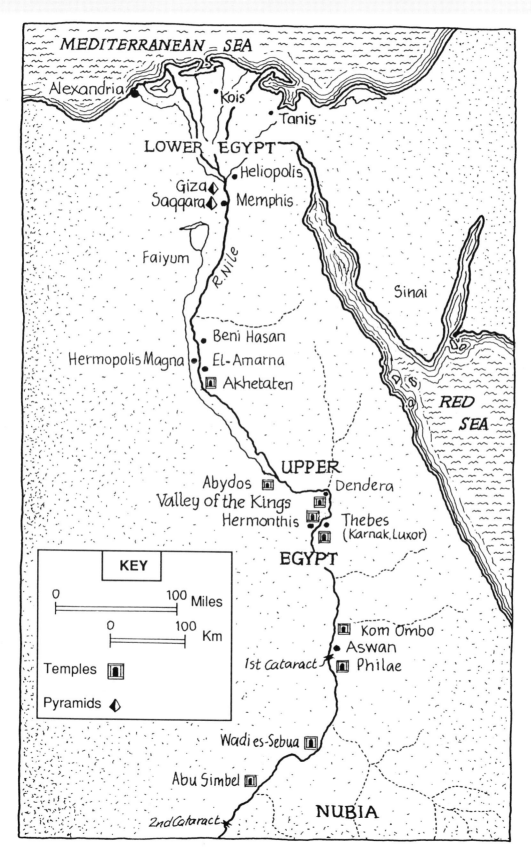

A TEMPLE

The temple at Edfu was dedicated to Horus, the falcon-headed god, son of Osiris and Isis. A temple was the home of the god; it was fed, clothed and looked after by the priests who were given their power by the Pharaoh.

Temples followed the same plan. The rooms became smaller and darker, and the floors higher as the shrine was approached.

Label the plan using the names and information below.

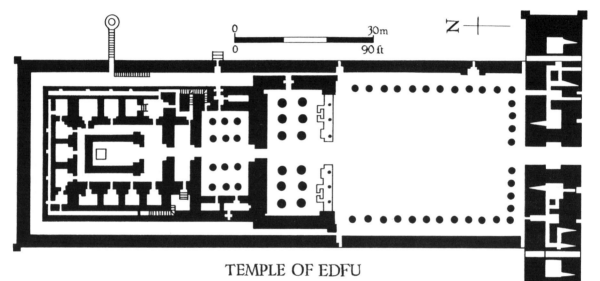

TEMPLE OF EDFU

SANCTUARY At the heart of the temple. Only priests and the King were allowed in. Rooms were smaller, darker, and higher.	**SHRINE** Sacred statue of the God kept in here. The very highest, darkest and most sacred area of the temple.	**NILOMETER** Monitored the level of the Nile before and after the inundation. Shows how closely the temple was associated with agriculture.	**OUTER CORRIDOR** A walking area where the walls were covered with reliefs telling religious stories.
PYLON Greek word for 'entrance'. Ceremonial entrances, niches at the top of the walls for huge flag poles.	**OPEN COURTYARD** Stood open to the sky before entering the darker secret hallway to the god.	**HYPOSTYLE HALL** Roofed, columned, darker hall. Symbolic of the papyrus swamp from which the world arose.	**PURIFICATION ROOMS** Tiny rooms either side of doorway just before hypostyle hall where priests prepared themselves to enter the presence of the god.

THE TOMB

Here is a plan of Tutankhamun's tomb - the smallest in the Valley of the Kings. Research in groups which rooms the treasures were found in and then label the diagram. Remember Howard Carter's words, when asked if he could see anything through the gloom: 'Yes, wonderful things ...'

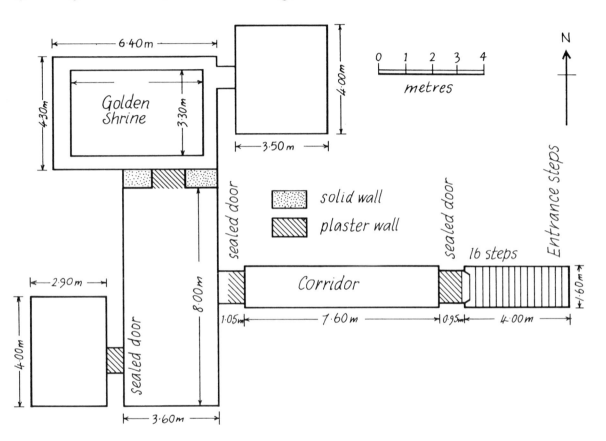

TREASURY	ANNEXE
East of the burial chamber. Had been entered by thieves but contained most valuable jewels, and the canopic jars containing the internal organs of the King. Entrance guarded by statue of Anubis.	Smaller and even more disordered room to the west. 'Not a single square inch of floor remains vacant,' said Carter. Contained many things but most importantly low beds, a throne, baskets of dried fruit and seeds, gaming boards.
ANTECHAMBER	**BURIAL CHAMBER**
Leading on from the corridor. Packed with furniture, boxes and vases thrown on top of one another by robbers who had been disturbed. 125 objects in all. Most precious objects included three gilded beds with carved animal heads, a trumpet, golden chariots, two lifesize golden Ka statues against a plastered wall to the north.	To north of the antechamber. Almost completely filled with the golden shrine. Four box-like shrines, one inside the other, contained the stone sarcophagus. Inside this were three mummiform coffins one inside the other, two of gilded wood, one of solid gold (110.4kg). Wrapped mummy inside wearing the death mask. 143 jewels distributed all over the body, which was in a bad state of preservation.

This page may be photocopied for classroom use only

HIEROGLYPHS

The Ancient Egyptians used a very different kind of alphabet. It consisted of over 700 signs or pictures called hieroglyphs. Scribes, whose job it was to write and record, learned these signs and pictures from childhood. They knew how to put them together to communicate.

Be a scribe and write messages. Use the chart containing just a few of the hieroglyphs, to write your own name in the cartouche - the oval shape drawn for you.

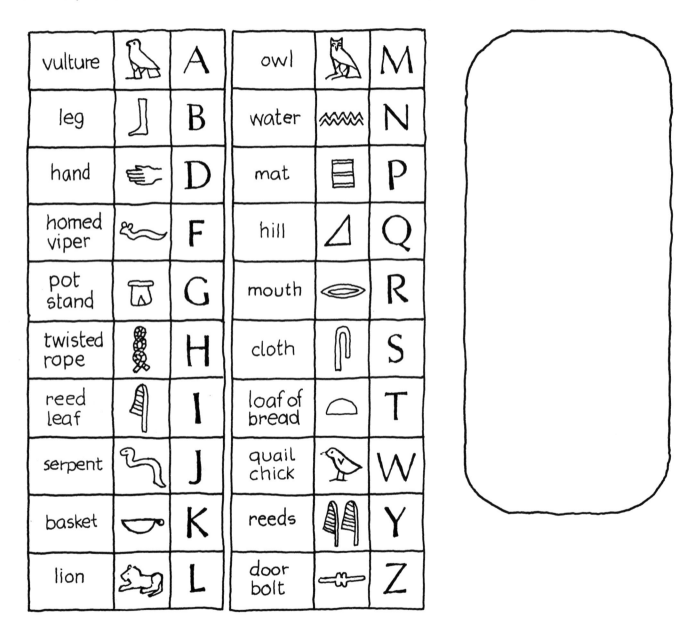

There were few vowels, but the sounds of the words were still communicated:
John would be written **JN** - serpent and water.